THE PRINCE OF MARTYRS

First published by
George Ronald

© A. Q. FAIZÍ 1977

ISBN 0 85398 073 X

EXTRACTS FROM THE FOLLOWING WORKS
REPRINTED BY PERMISSION:

By Bahá'u'lláh: *The Kitáb-i-Íqán*: The Book of Certitude, Copyright 1950 by National Spiritual Assembly of the Bahá'ís of the United States. By 'Abdu'l-Bahá: *Some Answered Questions*, Copyright 1930, 1954, © 1964 by National Spiritual Assembly of the Bahá'ís of the United States.

The cover photograph was kindly supplied by the Audio-Visual Department of the Bahá'í World Centre.

Set in 13 on 14 point Bembo

THE
PRINCE OF MARTYRS

a brief account of the
IMÁM ḤUSAYN

by

Abu'l-Qásim Faizí

GR

GEORGE RONALD
OXFORD

. . . For no warrior could be found on earth more excellent and nearer to God than Ḥusayn, son of 'Alí, so peerless and incomparable was he. "There was none to equal or to match him in the world." Yet, thou must have heard what befell him. God's malison on the head of the people of tyranny!

Furthermore, call to mind the shameful circumstances that have attended the martyrdom of Ḥusayn. Reflect upon his loneliness, how, to outer seeming, none could be found to aid him, none to take up his body and bury it. And yet, behold how numerous, in this day, are those who from the uttermost corners of the earth don the garb of pilgrimage, seeking the site of his martyrdom, that there they may lay their heads upon the threshold of his shrine! Such is the ascendancy and power of God! Such is the glory of His dominion and majesty!

Think not that because these things have come to pass after Ḥusayn's martyrdom, therefore all this glory hath been of no profit unto him. For that holy soul is immortal, liveth the life of God, and abideth within the retreats of celestial glory upon the Sadrih of heavenly reunion. These Essences of being are the shining Exemplars of sacrifice. They have offered, and will continue to offer up their lives, their substance, their souls, their spirit, their all, in the path of the Well-Beloved. By them, no station, however exalted, could be more dearly cherished. For lovers have no desire but the good-pleasure of their Beloved, and have no aim except re-union with Him.

Should We wish to impart unto thee a glimmer of the mysteries of Ḥusayn's martyrdom, and reveal unto thee the fruits thereof, these pages could never suffice, nor exhaust their meaning. Our hope is that, God willing, the breeze of mercy may blow, and the divine Spring-time clothe the tree of being with the robe of a new life; so that we may discover the mysteries of divine Wisdom, and, through His providence, be made independent of the knowledge of all things. . . . Therefore, know thou of a certainty that these Luminaries of heavenly majesty, though their dwelling be in the dust, yet their true habitation is the seat of glory in the realms above. Though bereft of all earthly possessions, yet they soar in the realms of immeasurable riches. And whilst sore tried in the grip of the enemy, they are seated on the right hand of power and celestial dominion. Amidst the dark-ness of their abasement there shineth upon them the light of unfading glory, and upon their helplessness are showered the tokens of an invincible sovereignty.

BAHÁ'U'LLÁH
from *The Kitáb-i-Íqán*

To write about a man whose martyrdom fortified the foundations of the Islamic Faith, whose blood cleansed the religion of his Grandfather of the detrimental traces of the spirit of the Age of Ignorance,[1] the mere mention of whose name creates waves of poignant sorrow in the hearts of his followers, whose personality towers above even the best of the Imáms, and whose station is so exalted that the hopes and aspirations of the true believers are centred on his "return", is a difficult undertaking. It is particularly difficult, since so little is known in the West of this incomparable figure, and that little vitiated by prejudicial accounts devoid of true judgement.

Like the waves of a stormy sea the turbulent events of history constantly surge and swirl, and we are astounded to witness that, amidst the manifold historical episodes associated with the early days of Islám, the most ardent believers, avowed supporters and staunch defenders of the new Faith of Muḥammad were put to the test, fell and vanished in that tempestuous ocean. "In a distant age and climate the tragic scene of the death of Hosein will

[1] *Jáhilíyyah*, before the advent of Muḥammad.

awaken the sympathy of the coldest reader",[1] and indeed, even in that bitter first century of Islám, his death evoked the greatest feeling of sorrow. The martyrdom of Ḥusayn did not occur as a sudden and spontaneous combustion. Nor should we consider it as a simple act of the murder of an individual. It took place as the consequence of deep-rooted animosities and prolonged struggles between the powers of darkness and the army of light.

One must study this tragedy with much devotion and patience. To obtain just a fragmentary outline of the decisive events which so altered the development of Islám, one must look back to the Age of Ignorance, gather the ends of as many threads as possible, and trace their course through the history of Arabia and Islám before and after the Prophet Muḥammad, thus detecting various causes of many of the events recorded. One must also stand at an adequate distance to see how deeply-rooted human weaknesses are manifested, how swords are substituted for words, how conquests lead to decline and everlasting fall, and how the sacred blood of devoted adherents is shed to open the way to the ultimate victory of the Word of God.

Though this deathless chapter of world history, which revolves around the central figure of Imám

[1] Gibbon, *The Decline and Fall of the Roman Empire*, ch. 50.

Ḥusayn, is unlimited in scope and fathomless in depth, it is nevertheless worthwhile to attempt a study of one who merits both our reverence and love. Bahá'u'lláh, the Báb, and 'Abdu'l-Bahá[1] all made numerous references to the acts of devotion and sacrifice of Imám Ḥusayn, and we find a special visitation prayer revealed for him by Bahá'u'lláh.

This essay is not intended to be exhaustive in scope. It is only a humble attempt to facilitate the study of the Imám's life and achievements. In these events will be found great feats of spiritual ardour and acts of self-sacrifice, the contemplation of which cannot but consolidate one's own faith.

The following outline of persons and happenings will, it is hoped, aid the reader to identify the individuals who played prominent parts in this tragedy and to follow the events in their proper order.

Persons and Events

1. The two outstanding clans of the Quraysh tribe in Mecca
   (a) The clan of Háshim
   (b) The clan of Umayyah

[1] Bahá'u'lláh (1817-92) was the Founder of the Bahá'í Faith, the Báb (1819-50) its Forerunner, and 'Abdu'l-Bahá (1844-1921) its Exemplar.

2. The first four Caliphs (A.D. 632–61)
   (a) Abú-Bakr
   (b) 'Umar
   (c) 'Uthmán
   (d) 'Alí
3. Mu'áwíyah, Governor of Syria, in Damascus, and the first Umayyad ruler (A.D. 661–80)
   (a) He stood against 'Alí.
   (b) After the assassination of 'Alí he caused 'Alí's son, Hasan, to withdraw and retire, and him-self became head of the Islamic Community.
   (c) He tried to obtain an oath of allegiance for his son Yazíd to succeed him, instead of Hasan's younger brother Husayn, to whom he had promised the succession.
4. Husayn, the third Imám (after 'Alí and Hasan)
   (a) On the death of Mu'áwíyah, he refused to acknowledge Yazíd's succession.
   (b) He was promised support by the people of Kúfah in Mesopotamia ('Iráq).
   (c) With a small band of about seventy followers and his family, he set out from Mecca in Hijáz for Kúfah.
   (d) Ibn Zíyád was the newly-appointed Governor of Kúfah.
   (e) Husayn's way was blocked by Hurr, a cavalry commander who, at Karbilá, joined

Ḥusayn's small company.

(f) Ibn Sa'd commanded the army of 4000 sent against Ḥusayn.

(g) On the plain of Karbilá Ḥusayn pitched his tents.

5. Ḥusayn's martyrdom, the 10th day of Muḥarram, 61 A.H. (October, A.D. 680)

(a) In the ensuing battle, Ḥusayn lost all the male members of his family and companions except his invalid son 'Alí, known as Zaynu'l-'Ábidín.

(b) Shimr was the shameless enemy who decapitated the Imám.

(c) Ḥusayn's body was trampled by horses.

(d) His son 'Alí, and the women and children, were taken captive and conducted, with the heads of their martyrs carried aloft on spears, to Kúfah from whence they were sent to Damascus.

(e) Yazíd sent the family from Damascus to Medina with the heads of their martyrs, which they buried in Karbilá forty days after the battle.

(f) This tragic event marked the final separation of the spiritual and administrative centres of the Islamic Faith.

The Ka'bah was the first house of worship ever erected in Arabia. It was built by Abraham, aided by his son Ishmael.[1] When they had finished the construction of this cube-like building, they prayed that God would accept their act of service. In the course of centuries, the House became a centre where many idols were placed and preserved by the tribes, each of which had several gods or goddesses to worship. To make the pilgrimage to Mecca was indeed for the sole purpose of worshipping the idols. This pilgrimage had many different stages to be performed over a number of days, and each stage was characterized by rituals, customs and habits which reflected the barbarous life of the Age of Ignorance prevalent in much of the Arabian peninsula.

There were several clans of the Quraysh who were responsible for the care of the pilgrims. The most prominent of their responsibilities were two: (1) The custodianship of the Ka'bah and the keeping of its key; and (2) The administration of Mecca and the provision of water for the pilgrims. Both responsibilities had been vested, in the latter half of the fifth century, in Quṣayy, but on his death authority was divided, the second responsibility

[1] Tradition has it that Adam built the Ka'bah, which was rebuilt in a later age by Abraham and Ishmael.

going to his grandson, 'Abd-Shams, the progenitor of the Umayyads, then passing to his brother Háshim, founder of the Háshimites. This transfer of authority, which engendered ill feelings of rivalry and jealousy between the two clans, became the starting-point of accusations, calumnies, petty strifes and skirmishes which were to stain the pages of Muslim history.

Háshim (d. 510) had been wealthy, generous and of good breeding, as were most of his descendants. But Abú-Sufyán, a merchant in olives and wool, and head of the Umayyads at the time of Muhammad, was notorious for his infamous character. The popularity of Háshim's descendants could not be endured by Abú-Sufyán. As the years went by, strong feelings of jealous rivalry mounted in his heart. Once such loathsome seeds are sown, they begin to grow and gradually become a deep-rooted tree the bitter fruits of which are consumed by the members of the tribe. Not only did the elders of Abú-Sufyán's family carry grudges against the Háshimites, but their children also began to hate them. At first, such differences remained within the small circle of Meccan life, but before long their frustrations and ill feelings gushed forth like a flood, inundating all aspects of Muslim life in Arabia and the neighbouring countries.

Now it happened that Muḥammad was singled out by God to act as His Messenger to mankind, and He was of the Háshimites. As His mission began to win adherents, the other clans of the Quraysh, fearing the ultimate victory of the Prophet, rose to persecute Him, His family, His followers and His nascent Faith. The members of Abú-Sufyán's family, under the direction, instigation and evil plotting of their chief, stood impervious to the truth and remained firm against the progress of Islám. So unbearable became the conditions for Muḥammad and His followers that some were forced to leave their country for Ethiopia, and soon thereafter the Muslims had to retire to a solitary valley outside Mecca, while the Meccans were commanded by their leaders to abstain from all trade with them. This state of affairs lasted for three years.

Eventually the Prophet decided to change His place of residence from Mecca to Medina, where He was welcomed by a band of followers. With the zeal and enthusiasm of new recruits, the believers won many to His side and soon the Prophet had an army of adherents under His command.

At length he decided to cleanse the House of God in Mecca, to awaken the Meccans to recognize the dawn of a new day, and to help them understand the truth of Islám and the influence it would have in the world, especially in Arabia which was still under the sway of the abhorred Age of Ignorance.

As the Prophet and His followers approached Mecca in an alarming march of triumph, the very first to embrace Islám was Abú-Sufyán; he was soon followed by the members of his family and a majority of the tribe of Quraysh.

Thus the germ of dissension, which had actively opposed the progress of the Faith of Islám, now entered the body of the Cause of God. It remained hidden but ever ready to emerge, like a virulent disease, to sap the spiritual vitality and strength of the religion of God—that tender young tree, drain enthusiasm and weaken religious affiliation, affect many of the pillars of Islám, put to the test groups of courageous adherents causing them to fail, and, above all, to divide the all-commanding and united power of the newly-established Faith of God. Its evil spell, once cast upon the divine institutions, brought many incorrigible individuals to absolute and ruthless power. Hypocrites found a ready arena for their wicked and arrogant schemes. Military conquests were substituted for spiritual conquests. The ordinances, precepts and intensely spiritual exhortations of Islám gave way to the spirit and the rules of life prevalent in the Age of Ignorance. And the religion of God became as a dead body deprived even of burial.[1] There was need of a supreme sacrifice to create those mysterious energies which draw people near to their Creator and closer to His religion and His plan for mankind.

Ḥusayn, the grandson of the Prophet, was destined to give the blood of his family and himself for such a spiritual regeneration.

At the death of the Prophet, that poisonous germ began to manifest its evil effects, and its contamination weakened the faith of even the most renowned champions of Islám. It is related that the Prophet, returning home from His last pilgrimage, had gathered His followers together and orally but emphatically designated 'Alí as their master. His mission, He had told them in Mecca, was completed. When he became ill and was bed-ridden, His closest and most stalwart supporters were in His room. He asked for paper and pen to dictate that which would keep them united. "The man is in delirium," said one of them; "sufficient to us is the Book of God." These words were to cause a disastrous

[1] See 'Abdu'l-Bahá, *Some Answered Questions*, ch. XI. (Bahá'í Publishing Trust, Wilmette, Illinois, rev. edn. 1964.)

schism in the religion of God that remained irreparable and continually widened as the years went on.

The moment the Prophet laid His head to rest, 'Alí—His cousin and the husband of His illustrious daughter Fáṭimah, who was the second to believe in Him and was the embodiment of nobility, audacity and justice—was left alone to arrange the burial of the Prophet, while those who had heard the penetrating voice of the Prophet on the day He announced 'Alí as their master gathered in another place to initiate their own plan, not according to His words, but in accord with the rules of the tribes. Thus the positive forces were robbed of their powers and prerogatives, while the negative ones ruled throughout the decades and centuries.[1] Heedless of this event, which is recorded by almost all the chroniclers of the birth of Islám, many outstanding historians, even those who are Muslims, have disregarded this critical point, creating so many doubts with their own interpretations that the mirror of historical fact has become obscured and darkened.

The tumultuous and heated discussion which ensued, in the effort to choose a successor to their Prophet, was appeased by the disinterested reso-

[1] See *Gleanings from the Writings of Bahá'u'lláh*, section xxiii. (Bahá'í Publishing Trust, Wilmette, Illinois, rev. edn. 1952.)

lution of 'Umar, who, "suddenly renouncing his own pretensions, stretched forth his hand, and declared himself the first subject of the mild and venerable"[1] Abú-Bakr. This act was described by Gibbon as an "illegal and precipitate measure".

Abú-Bakr, after a rule of two years, designated 'Umar as his successor. 'Umar conquered and ruled for ten years and, before his death, nominated six men from whom one should be chosen to succeed him. 'Uthmán was named by that council.

When 'Uthmán took the reins of affairs in his feeble hands, he appointed the members of his family to be governors of states and judges of provinces. He was a descendant of Umayyah like Abú-Sufyán, and thus the most important office of the Islamic world came under the sway of the Umayyads. 'Uthmán, because of his practice of nepotism, was disliked by the people, and his "feeble temper and declining age . . . were incapable of sustaining the weight of conquest and empire". From many parts of the Islamic world delegations were sent to 'Uthmán, to plead with him to exercise justice. Failing to do so, he was assassinated in his own house. "A tumultuous anarchy of five days was appeased by the inauguration of Ali: his refusal would have provoked a general massacre," al-

[1] Gibbon, op. cit.

though 'Alí "declared that he had rather serve than reign". Twenty-four years after the death of the Prophet, the Islamic world acclaimed Imám 'Alí as its leader, and he "was invested, by the popular choice, with the regal and sacerdotal office".[1]

"The birth, the alliance, the character of Ali, which exalted him above the rest of his countrymen, might justify his claim to the vacant throne of Arabia," Gibbon has observed. "The son of Abu Taleb was, in his own right, the chief of the family of Hashem, and the hereditary prince or guardian of the city and temple of Mecca. The light of prophecy was extinct; but the husband of Fatima might expect the inheritance and blessing of her father;" who spoke of him as "vicegerent" and even referred to him as the "Aaron of a second Moses". His two sons, Ḥasan and Ḥusayn, had been very often on the lap of the Prophet receiving special love and were called "the chief of the youth of paradise". "He united the qualifications of a poet, a soldier, and a saint: his wisdom still breathes in a collection of moral and religious sayings;[2] and every antagonist,

[1] The passages quoted in this paragraph and the next are from Gibbon, op. cit.
[2] The collection is called *Nahju'l-Balághah*, and is referred to by the great teachers of Islám as "not the words of the Creator, but heaven above the words of man".

in the combats of the tongue or of the sword, was subdued by his eloquence and valour."

In the words of Professor Hitti: "Valiant in battle, wise in counsel, eloquent in speech, true to his friends, magnanimous to his foes, he became both the paragon of Moslem nobility and chivalry . . . and the Solomon of Arabic tradition, around whose name poems, proverbs, sermonettes and anecdotes innumerable have clustered. He had a swarthy complexion, large black eyes, bald head, thick and long white beard, and was corpulent and of medium stature. His sabre dhu-al-Faqār (the cleaver of vertebrae), . . . has been immortalized in the words of the verse found engraved on many medieval Arab swords . . . 'No sword can match dhu-al-Faqār, and no young warrior can compare with 'Ali !' "[1]

The people knew him as a true believer in Islám, one who would keep to its spirit and never deviate even a hair's breadth from the right path of God. His way of life was simple; he despised the vanities of the world. He showed no favouritism. Even his own brother abandoned him when he received no extra share from the revenues, for 'Alí spared no

[1] Philip K. Hitti, *History of the Arabs*, p. 183. (Macmillan and Co. Ltd, London, 10th edn. 1970; also St. Martin's Press, Inc., New York.)

effort to protect the treasury of the Faith from plunder by covetous individuals.

With the vigour of an undaunted hero and ruler, and the unsurpassed determination of a spiritual leader, he began to purify the administrative institutions of Islám and to dismiss those who were unworthy of position. He wrote beautiful letters to the governors, breathing into them the true spirit of the Faith, and reminding them of the Prophet's lofty standard of justice and tolerance towards the followers of all religions. By such firm steps in the purification of all the channels of affairs, 'Alí conquered the hearts of the people of Mecca; and when they were agitated by the activities of his opponents, he recited the verses of God with so much strength and calmness and in such a spirit of self-sacrifice that they came to know his magnanimity in peace, as they had known his valour and audacity in war. On many hazardous occasions, he manifested such determination and truthfulness that the cunning plots of his adversaries were averted and frustrated.

But the Quraysh, in the words of Gibbon, "could never be reconciled to the proud pre-eminence of the line of Hashem: and the ancient discord of the tribes was rekindled." Indeed, in all the phases of the history of Islám, we observe the traces of discord and animosity which started in the Age of Ignorance, penetrating into the very core of the Muslim institutions and dividing the loyalty of the rank and file of its adherents. Like the deadening winds of autumn, disunity swept through all domains and caused the weakening, failure and fall of many of the followers of Islám. "The mischiefs that flow from the contests of ambition are usually confined to the times and countries in which they have been agitated. But the religious discord of the friends and enemies of Ali has been renewed in every age" of Islamic history.[1] Periodical clashes of an intense nature between the army of light and the powers of darkness were one by one unfolded and in all of them we find 'Alí and his illustrious descendants victims in the merciless clutches of the Umayyads.

The Muslim world was shocked when it heard that two influential leaders, aided and accompanied by 'Á'ishah, the wife of the Prophet, had waged war against 'Alí. Upon their defeat, and the death of the two leaders, 'Alí proved most magnanimous. He mourned the deaths of his brave adversaries and the "venerable captive . . . was speedily dismissed to her proper station, at the

[1] Passages quoted in this paragraph and the next are from Gibbon, op. cit.

tomb of Mahomet, with the respect and tenderness that was still due to the widow of the apostle".

But the most formidable of 'Alí's opponents was in Damascus. Mu'áwíyah, son of Abú-Sufyán, had been appointed by his relative 'Uthmán as governor of Syria. With an insatiable thirst for still higher rank and position, an intense desire to exterminate the last traces of the Háshimites, and motivated by an unmitigated hatred of 'Alí, Mu'áwíyah stood resolutely against the man to whom the Muslim world had promised fidelity and obedience. Mu'áwíyah's intention was to establish himself as Caliph of Islám and to secure for his descendants the throne of a dynasty. He moved against 'Alí, who, by his heroic deeds, had almost won the day, when suddenly he was "compelled to yield to a disgraceful truce and an insidious compromise".[1]

After the assassination of 'Alí, in the mosque of Kúfah, Mu'áwíyah had a supreme opportunity to widen the range of his perfidious activities throughout the Muslim domains. He retained the name of Islám as an outer garment, while ceaselessly pouring out his venom of rivalry and jealousy against the Háshimites. Emboldened by the gap created by 'Alí's murder, he revealed his own schemes by

[1] Gibbon, op. cit.

vilifying 'Alí in the mosques, minarets and markets. Preachers who would invent traditions against 'Alí were promoted and received gifts of immense value. Those who expressed love and loyalty toward 'Alí and his family were put to death in cruel and insidious ways. Honey mixed with poison was often used. Mu'áwíyah would always say that the army of God is in honey.

Ḥasan, the eldest son of 'Alí, was acclaimed as his successor, but soon he was forced by Mu'áwíyah to withdraw and retire. He was at last poisoned by a slave girl named Ja'dih who poured diamond powder into the Imám's jar of water. She committed this unforgiveable sin because of Mu'áwíyah's promise to give her gold coins and arrange her marriage to his son Yazíd, promises which were never fulfilled.

Thus the son of Abú-Sufyán, who had put forth all his efforts to stop the forward progress of the religion of God, was now settled on his throne by ruse and cunning. His nefarious activities were underscored by a now-famous motto attributed to him. "'I apply not my sword,' he is reported to have declared, 'where my lash suffices, nor my lash where my tongue is enough. And even if there be one hair binding me to my fellow men, I do not let it break: when they pull I loosen, and if they loosen

I pull.'"[1] By giving the people gold, lands and promises of high position, he drew to his court in Damascus persons who were as pillars of Islám; they were put to tests which many failed. He tried by all means to attract men to his court, and threatened those who showed reluctance to approach. He confiscated properties, gouged out the eyes of those who refused to co-operate, hanged them, buried them alive. Such nefarious acts have led certain historians, lacking in judgement and insight, to acclaim Mu'áwíyah as the truest and shrewdest politician of the Arabian peninsula.

We come now to the sad story of that matchless soul, the third Imám, Ḥusayn. As long as his elder brother Ḥasan was alive, Ḥusayn obeyed him as a true believer. But when Ḥasan died, it was Ḥusayn's right and privilege to protect his succession to the Caliphate, and his function as the third Imám. It was one of his sayings that should the Faith of his Grandfather require blood to fortify its spiritual foundations, he was ever ready to offer his own.

Mu'áwíyah knew very well that his own son Yazíd would not easily be accepted by the people of

[1] Hitti, *The Arabs, A Short History*, pp. 59–60. (Macmillan, London, 5th edn. 1968; also St. Martin's Press, New York.)

Ḥijáz and 'Iráq as their Caliph. Therefore, during his own lifetime, he tried to arrange affairs in such a way as to facilitate Yazíd's succession to the throne of the Caliphate. His concern was not that there should be a true successor of the Prophet, one who could be the supreme spiritual example to his people. Rather, his sole aim was to establish a powerful dynasty of his own family, whose domains would rival in scope and wealth the Persian and Roman Empires. But his instruction to the governor of Medina, to obtain pledges of allegiance to Yazíd from Ḥusayn and several other notables, did not succeed before his death.

Yazíd then attempted to obtain submission to his rule, particularly from Ḥusayn and one other notable, and dispatched to Walíd, the governor of Medina, strict orders to this effect. Walíd had no alternative but to summon them, but only Ḥusayn went to the governor's house. There was a man in Walíd's *entourage* named Marwán. He was an insidious and wicked plotter, who, though a professed Muslim, spied for the infidels. According to the writer of *Muḥriqu'l-Qulúb*[1] he was a dangerous element in the province of Ḥijáz, inspiring evil

---

[1] The book read in the presence of the Báb in the prison of Máh-Kú. See Nabíl, *The Dawn-Breakers*, p. 252. (Bahá'í Publishing Trust, Wilmette, Illinois, 1932.)

deeds by his whisperings, promptings and sugges-
tions. As Ḥusayn entered the governor's room,
Marwán was sitting there, quiet and malignant as a
dead mouse. Ḥusayn asked Walíd about the purpose
of his invitation. When the governor disclosed to
him the orders he had received from Damascus,
Ḥusayn frankly and boldly exclaimed that such
oaths should be taken in the mosque and in the
presence of the Muslim community, never in
private. Having said this, he turned to leave. Marwán whispered to Walíd to capture the Imám
immediately, but Walíd ignored this prompting,
for he harboured in his heart a certain respect for the
family of the Apostle of God.

The idea of obtaining an oath of allegiance from
Ḥusayn was pursued by Yazíd with unflagging
industry and obstinate ignorance. Such an oath of
loyalty by Ḥusayn would have wrapped the dead
body of the Faith of God in shrouds of oblivion,
and rung a death-knell for the hopes and aspirations
of the true believers. But the forces of light remain
forever victorious and never reconcilable with the
powers of darkness.

Ḥusayn had left the governor's house in Medina
for his own, but his mind grappled with deeply
disturbing thoughts and poignant sorrows, for he
realized that the fate of the religion of Islám was

hanging in the balance. To save the covenant of God from irretrievable loss, he decided to go from Medina to Mecca.

It was strange indeed that a perverted and corrupt man such as Yazíd should presume to claim the mantle of the Prophet when his shoulders were already heavily burdened with sins. Harder still is it to think of a drunkard occupying the position of the Prophet, leading the believers at times of prayer and inviting them to the path of spiritual accomplishment. So addicted was he to alcoholic beverages that he could not abstain from drinking, even in the few days of his pilgrimage to Mecca.

Yazíd was absorbed in the frivolities and luxuries of life and was very keen on hunting. He remained oblivious to the fact that his domains were seething with discontent and on the brink of revolt. Imitating the heinous deeds of his father, he also employed many devilish means to achieve his aims. He used poison and fire and bribes, gifts, gold, positions and properties to corrupt the faithful, sheathe the swords of the brave, and silence those with eloquent tongues. He appointed the ignorant as teachers, the ill-famed as missionaries, and the cowards as commanders. A chilling and striking contrast to Ḥusayn! "The only quality that he lacked," says Sédillot, "was the spirit of intrigue which characterised the descendants of Ommeya."[1]

Ḥusayn was aware of the deep-rooted hatred festering in the hearts of the Umayyads. He noticed that they multiplied their chains of control and strengthened them by drawing to their side prominent people in the Islamic world. To enlarge their dominions and to hold them more strictly under their own surveillance, they offered highly-coveted prizes. Even some of the Háshimites joined their ranks, for the temptations were greater than they could resist.

Perplexing news, manifold and magnified, was reaching the court of Yazíd. He sent a special envoy to Mecca to control the pilgrimage. But the pilgrims were attracted to Ḥusayn. As the grandson of their Prophet and in his own right a man of irresistible charm and regal dignity, they acclaimed him with love and reverence beyond the measure of expectation. Yazíd received this news, and the volcano of hatred and jealousy which smouldered within his heart erupted in a stream of awesome calamities directed at Ḥusayn. The sole aim of the tyrant of Syria was to obtain a pledge of obedience from this unique man who was so highly revered by the Muslim world.

[1] Cited by Syed Ameer Ali in *A Short History of the Saracens*, pp. 83-4. (Macmillan & Co. Ltd., London, repr. 1921.)

When the news reached 'Iráq, the Muslims, especially those in the city of Kúfah, who in the words of Ameer Ali were "Eager, fierce, and impetuous, [but] . . . utterly wanting in persever-ance and steadiness",[1] decided to invite Ḥusayn to their own country and to acclaim him as the third Imám to whom all would remain loyal and obedient. They wrote literally thousands of letters and dispatched them to Mecca, promising their absolute loyalty. In the midst of their excitement, there was one man who addressed the people of Kúfah, begging them to think well before swearing such oaths of fidelity, and not to stake the precious life of Ḥusayn on the venture. But the streams of signed and sealed letters bearing their promises con-tinued to flow to Mecca.

Ḥusayn decided to accept their invitations. Many close friends and even his younger brother advised him not to rely on the inhabitants of 'Iráq and their pledges. They proposed that, if he intended to go away, he should choose Yemen where the followers of the Prophet were steadfast and truthful. Some of the tribesmen of the desert also warned him against the people of Kúfah, saying, "Their hearts may be with you, but their spears and swords will be against you." A Shaykh asked Ḥusayn where he would go.

[1] ibid., p. 84.

On hearing his reply, "To Kúfah", in great agony the Shaykh exlaimed, "They will receive you on the points of their lances and the edges of their swords". But Ḥusayn was undaunted by danger, choosing to tread the path most acceptable to his Lord and Creator.

The night before his departure Ḥusayn was in profound meditation, his mind filled with a host of recollections. He knew that he would never look again on the scenes associated with his Grandfather, the Apostle of God; with 'Alí, the ever-conquering lion of God; and with Fáṭimah, his mother, who had been singled out by Alláh as peerless among women in the Islamic Dispensation. In the ominous calmness of that night countless memories overwhelmed his sanctified heart. In the all-enveloping darkness, he balanced the behests of his heart and the formidable commands of destiny. Should he choose to stay in Ḥijáz, it would mean taking an oath of obedience to the throne of the despot of Damascus. Such an action would carry Islám to utter destruction. He knew that he could never leave the straight path of his destiny, though it be flooded with adversities and surrounded by calamities. In the words of Gibbon, "The primogeniture of the line of Hashem, and the holy character of grandson of the apostle, had centered in his person, and he was at liberty to prosecute his claim against Yezid, the tyrant of Damascus, whose vices he despised, and whose title he had never deigned to acknowledge."

Yazíd, aware of the imminent dangers smouldering in 'Iráq, could visualize the ruin of himself and his dynasty. He began to prepare his soldiers and commanders to commit the most nefarious deeds in his favour. Next he approached Ibn Zíyád, and sent him to replace the unhappy governor of Kúfah. Ibn Zíyád "was at first styled ibn-Abīh [the son of his father] because of the doubt which clouded the identity of his father. His mother was a slave and prostitute in al-Ṭā'if whom abu-Sufyān, Mu'āwiyah's father, had known. Ziyād was pro-'Alid.[1] In a critical moment Mu'āwiyah acknowledged Ziyād as his legitimate brother."[2] Upon receiving Yazíd's commission, Ibn Zíyád seized his new responsibility with vigour, malice and inflexible cruelty. He entered the city of Kúfah with his face covered and wearing a black turban resembling that of the family of 'Alí. At first the inhabitants of Kúfah took him for Imám Ḥusayn whose arrival they all expected. But when, in the house of the governor, Ibn Zíyád uncovered his face, they realized they were in the presence of the newly-appointed governor of

[1] In favour of 'Alí and his claim to be the first Imám. (A.-Q.F.)
[2] Hitti, History of the Arabs, p. 196.

the eastern provinces of the Islamic Empire.

On the morrow of his arrival, Ibn Zíyád ascended the pulpit and in a sudden burst of anger uttered such brazen and terrifying words as to fill the hearts of the populace with horror and numbing fear. Brandishing his whip in one hand and his sword in the other, the new governor threatened to whip to death any who might dare to utter even as much as one word against the prevailing order; and to decapitate those who should venture the slightest gesture of disobedience. He then summoned the notables, the learned and the influential citizens of the town and promised them high positions and costly gifts. Within two days the inhabitants of 'Iráq were utterly overtaken by terror on the one hand and by greed on the other. They wavered, and abandoned their expected guest to the hands of his oppressors. Their hearts were changed, and discord and dissension became manifest in words and uncouth forms. Those who had invited Ḥusayn and assured him of their loyalty faltered and fled.

All these events took place while Ḥusayn was on his way to 'Iráq. Before reaching its hostile and inhospitable confines, he sent his faithful and audacious cousin, Muslim, to examine the situation. Soon Ibn Zíyád came to know of the arrival in

Kúfah of the Imám's envoy. His orders were strict
and urgent. A slave woman had given shelter and
food to Muslim, but how could anyone escape Ibn
Zíyád's miserable schemes? Muslim was soon
captured and dragged to the governor, who found
in his arrest an opportunity to strengthen his rule
and to establish in Kúfah his reign of terror. At his
behest Muslim was taken to the roof of a house, beheaded, and his corpse thrown down to be crushed
on the pavement. The action served its purpose.
Thereafter none dared even to think of love for
Ḥusayn, nor was Muslim able to alert the Imám to
the ambivalent attitude and infidelity of the people
of Kúfah, who had been totally won over to Yazíd
by his appointed governor in 'Iráq.

This done, Ibn Zíyád dispatched soldiers to
obstruct the roads to 'Iráq, Syria and Persia which
Ḥusayn might take. He even installed special
guards at wells so that Ḥusayn and his companions
would suffer from thirst, aggravated by the blazing
sun in the endless desert of Arabia.

He then singled out one of the finest and most
energetic of his young cavalry officers, by the name
of Ḥurr, and placed him at the head of a thousand
skilful soldiers to guard and prevent Ḥusayn from
approaching any town or village in 'Iráq, especially
the area surrounding Kúfah. Knowing the perils of

afflictive thirst, and aware of the scarcity of water in the desert, Ḥusayn had instructed his friends to store and carry as much water as they could. Ḥurr met the Imám on his way to 'Iráq, stopped him and explained why he and his soldiers were there. Ḥusayn, in turn, told Ḥurr of the invitations he had received from the people of Kúfah, and even showed him the bag containing more than ten thousand signed letters promising support and allegiance. Ḥurr exclaimed that he knew nothing about such communications and that his mission was to prevent Ḥusayn from advancing into 'Iráq. This marked the beginning of all the calamities which were to be heaped upon the grandson of the Prophet.

Ḥusayn had no desire to wage war. In his dismay and anxiety, he was overwhelmed by a sense of impending storm. He asked the young officer that he and his followers be allowed to settle anywhere in Arabia. Ḥurr, who had not the slightest desire to be stigmatized as the one to cause difficulties and suffering for the grandson of the Prophet, sent a message to Ibn Zíyád, informing him of the small band of companions of Ḥusayn and of their ex-pressed desire to settle in Arabia.

By this time, Ḥurr's own soldiers and horses were threatened by thirst. When the Imám came to know of this, he immediately provided them with water, generously giving them all that his companions had stored. This magnanimous gesture affected Ḥurr. When the time of prayer came, the commander and his soldiers stood in rows and followed the Imám in prayer.

Ḥusayn and his companions mounted their steeds and rode on, but Ḥurr maintained his watch and controlled their movements, never allowing them to take any road which would lead to the villages or towns of 'Iráq. Ḥusayn proceeded on until he reached the plain of Karbilá where he pitched his tents and settled. It was the second of Muḥarram[1] in the year 61 after Hijrah.

When Ibn Zíyád received Ḥurr's dispatch and realized that he had shown clemency towards and prayed with Ḥusayn, his rage knew no bounds. He immediately summoned 'Umar Ibn Sa'd and ordered him to prepare and equip an army of at least four thousand soldiers to encounter Ḥusayn and force him to sign a pledge of submission and obedience to Yazíd. He knew very well that for the early Muslims of Arabia, the promised paradise was the country of Persia. They would undergo endless hardships to reach there and settle in that verdant

---

[1] The birthday of Bahá'u'lláh, according to the lunar calendar, is the second of Muḥarram, in the year 1233 A.H. (after Hijrah).

region, which offered in abundance rivers, orchards, and a mild and desirable climate. Therefore Ibn Ziyád, after appointing Ibn Sa'd as chief commander of the army, promised him that in the event of success he would go to Persia as governor of Ray, the vast and prosperous province where the capital city of Ṭihrán stands to-day. Those who had sent letters of invitation to Ḥusayn and sworn fidelity to him became the allies of his enemies, rushing to arms in the hope of following their commander to the verdant lands of Persia.

Before the arrival of the newly-recruited and well-armed forces, Ḥusayn arose as a spiritual hero to face the inevitable. He gathered his followers, almost seventy in number,[1] and frankly disclosed to them the hardships and sufferings with which they would be afflicted. He pleaded with them to leave the plain of Karbilá for the peace and security of their own homes, and assured them they would never be considered infidels should they follow this counsel. Though filled with zest for life and sharing the common human aspirations for happiness and tranquillity, none of them abandoned the Imám, but remained firm and steadfast. They even expressed their joy at being able to share in the austerity and hardships of his existence, for they

[1] This number does not include the women and children.

longed to remain in his presence and under his loving leadership. To contribute to the Imám's pleasure and contentment was their highest goal.

The great army under Ibn Sa'd was startled on meeting Ḥusayn's small band. The Imám approached the commander-in-chief and discussed the situation with him. He insisted that he had not the slightest desire to shed the blood of anyone, and proposed that he should be left free to settle in peace in Arabia, be stationed on the borders of Turkey, or go to Damascus to meet Yazíd himself.

Ibn Sa'd, aspiring to become the ruler of Ray, emphatically replied that having entrapped him, they would never allow him out of their sight; his only solution would be to sign a pledge of explicit obedience to Yazíd. Well aware of Ḥusayn's irresistible charm and unyielding spirit, Ibn Zíyád sent at this time a contemptible beast in the person of Shimr, to ensure that Ibn Sa'd would not show respect and clemency towards the Imám.

Ḥusayn, in whatever condition he might find himself, would ceaselessly utter words of praise and adoration. Whether in happiness and prosperity, or in the midst of misfortune and adversity, he would offer thanksgiving to his Lord, and he often expressed particular gratitude for being a descendant of the Apostle of God, and enriched by the bounty of the Qur'án. He also thanked his Creator for the members of his family and his friends who, though few in number, demonstrated the most exalted spirit of faith, devotion and steadfastness.

Facing his companions, he prayed for them and supplicated God to grant them His rewards and number them among His near ones. As the eve of the tenth of Muḥarram approached, he addressed his followers and once more stressed that the army of Ibn Sa'd desired no one except himself. They were free to avail themselves of the darkness of the night to go in safety to their own homes and people. He even assured them that, should they choose to withdraw, they would never be counted among those who had broken the covenant of God.

"But this would leave us alive after you," was the unanimous reply of his devoted friends. "How could we ever pardon ourselves! To leave our beloved in the hands of ferocious beasts and save our own lives is abhorrent to us." And they all refused to abandon Ḥusayn alone in the midst of his foes.

Throughout that night, Ḥusayn could see the flickering shadows behind the screen of arms and he knew that the eventful day would soon dawn. He decided to exhort his adversaries again in the hope of a peaceful settlement. It was the path, he believed, which the Prophet Himself would have taken.

Once more he advanced towards the encampment of Ibn Sa'd and addressed him and his soldiers. His words, jewels of celestial truth, conveyed an enraptured vision of the bounty of God and drew to his side certain brave souls, who offered to mingle their blood with that of the Imám's heroic companions, to preserve themselves from breaking the covenant of God.

The most renowned of those repentant souls was the vigorous commander Ḥurr, who had obstructed all roads to Ḥusayn. His transformation took place in the depths of night, nor could his soldiers believe their eyes when they beheld this man of courage trembling like a leaf in a winter storm. "But we have never seen you in fear, even in the midst of the most terrifying battles," they cried. "I find myself between heaven and hell," was Ḥurr's reply. "My soul cries out and cannot bear these torments of hell." In the faint light of dawn, he charged his steed towards Ḥusayn, to express his penitence and beg forgiveness. When he had received the Imám's grace and assurance, he faced the army of Ibn Sa'd and chided them in loud tones, hoping to awaken their dormant souls. But alas! Those who were his comrades and under his command, attacked and killed him in an outburst of despicable ferocity.

Even water was denied to the Imám's small

band. The sight of the glimmering Euphrates in that barren and waterless desert aggravated their sufferings. Whoever approached the river for a drink, or ventured out to bring a container of water, became the target of spears and javelins.

This was the tragic fate of Ḥusayn's brother, 'Abbás, the standard-bearer of the Imám's camp, renowned as the most handsome of the Háshimites, and famed as the lion-hearted man of Arabia. In an audacious quest for water, he reached the Euphrates, filled his skin container, and charged his steed toward the tents where children were dying of thirst. Ibn Sa'd flew into a rage when he saw his orders flouted and challenged. His soldiers pursued 'Abbás ferociously, cut off his right hand, then his left, in which he carried the container, pierced its skin, and attacked and killed the water-carrier of Karbilá in a most atrocious way.

With an unswerving rectitude of character, unabated vigour and firmness, Ḥusayn persevered in his readiness to offer all that he possessed as a ransom for the Faith of his Grandfather. Carrying his youngest son who was in the cradle, he held him aloft and asked for water for that suckling child. An arrow lodged deep in the throat of the baby. Ḥusayn tossed the blood of his infant boy into the air. That precious child, it seems, was the last link which fastened his father to life on this planet. After sacrificing him, he became free as a bird, light as the breeze of the morning and ready to take his last flight to the celestial domain. Now, "alone, weary, and wounded, he seated himself at the door of his tents [where] he was pierced in the mouth with a dart."[1] This was indeed the bitterest moment of his life. He offered prayers for the dead and reflected upon the losses he had sustained. His sons, the son of his brother Ḥasan, the sons of his sister Zaynab, his followers and their sons—all had been killed in the bloom of their youth.

Vital questions must have flooded Ḥusayn's mind. What would happen to his dear son, Zaynu'l-'Ábidín, who was an invalid and confined to bed? What would be the fate of the women of his family at the hands of the merciless and bloodthirsty soldiers? Who could ever arrest the evil tide of events which was staining the soil of Karbilá? What path would be destined for the Faith of Islám when it fell totally under the sway of the tyrants of Damascus, the beasts from the desert?

At this, the darkest moment of his precious life, when portents and omens clouded his heart, he was ready to bear whatever blows might descend upon him. In his innermost heart he knew his love for

[1] Gibbon, op. cit.

God and was confident of God's never-failing triumphs, unblurred and unsullied. He arose as a spiritual giant to proclaim: "And verily Our host shall conquer".[1] It was a voice from the unknown which still resounds in that desert.

The valiant heroes of God advanced one by one and all were put to death. They were so uplifted by spiritual fervour that they longed for nothing but to offer their lives to safeguard the covenant of God.

By noontide of the tenth of Muḥarram not one of Ḥusayn's fighting-men remained. For his final words with the army of Ibn Sa'd, Ḥusayn advanced towards them and addressed them in his melodious voice. With conviction and love he exhorted the soldiers, reminded them of their letters to him, requested them to cease fighting and emphatically reiterated his appeal to withdraw from the scene of bloodshed. Individual soldiers were moved by his words and scarcely anyone dared to throw even a stone at him. The writer of *Muḥriqu'l-Qulúb* says that at this critical moment an arrow sank deep in Ḥusayn's body and then a thundering voice was heard. "Inform Ibn Zíyád that *I* was the first to shoot an arrow!" Such was the claim of the chief commander, Ibn Sa'd.

How contemptible and disgraceful are often the

[1] Qur'án 37: 173.

standards set by men! To take pride in killing the
grandson of the Prophet! To hope by this cowardly
act to win the approval of Ibn Zíyád!

This first arrow aimed at the Imám opened a
dam and released a flood which covered the plain
of Karbilá—land of agony and disaster—and carried
off the family and friends of Ḥusayn to captivity
and martyrdom. An army of more than four
thousand, to please the despots of Kúfah and
Damascus and to ensure their own share of the
booty of war, assailed seventy people and threatened their women and children. The army had
every available means; Ḥusayn's companions had
none. No supremacy of valour or audacity could be
claimed for that victory.

At noon Ḥusayn asked for a truce to say the noon
prayers, which was granted. He chanted prayers,
sang songs of heroism, and committed his family
to the loving care and ever-abiding protection of
God. As the hour of his death approached, an un-
bounded ecstasy transformed his pitiable plight and
found expression in words of joy and exultation.

After prayers, he again counselled his opponents
in gem-like words, but they surrounded him like
beasts of prey, striking so many blows with iron
bars, spears and swords that he could no longer
support himself on his charger and fell to the

ground. His horse galloped towards the tents where the Imám's family had taken shelter, paused there a little, then disappeared into the endless desert.

The full brunt of the wrath of that frantic mob fell heavily on the Imám. His face was streaming with blood. He lifted up his garment to wipe it away. In that moment an arrow sank deep in his chest, causing him to fall to his knees. The wounds were all on his chest and arms, for he never turned his back to his foes. Then a soldier gave the Imám such a severe blow on the head that he fell on his face.

In the confusion, a group of soldiers, headed by the heartless Shimr, started to invade the Imám's tents for the purpose of looting and putting all to death. Ḥusayn shouted at them, "If you do not follow the religion of God, behave, at least, as true Arabs, and spare the women and children!" Shimr turned back at once, ordering his soldiers to withdraw.

The hand of death was not yet on Ḥusayn, and although fallen he inspired such awe in the hearts of the soldiers that no one dared to commit the heinous deed of decapitating him. Some approached but shuddered in fear and rejoined their ranks. "The remorseless Shamer, a name detested by the faithful, reproached their cowardice."[1] Then this envoy of

[1] Gibbon, op. cit.

the governor of Kúfah fell like a thunderbolt on Ḥusayn's body and severed his head with nearly ten strokes. This sealed the contemptible victory of four thousand over barely seventy. No historian could rightly attribute it to superior intelligence, bravery or manhood. The episode remains as it was, an irremovable stain upon the history of mankind. Yet, in its exquisite demonstration of the gallantry of a few firm and steadfast adherents, it breathes courage and life even into bare bones, while its example of magnanimity awakens in those who justly consider it a desire to attain new heights of conscious and active devotion.

The martyrdom of Ḥusayn occurred at midday of Friday, the tenth of Muḥarram, the first month in the lunar calendar, in the year sixty-one after Hijrah.

The soldiers stripped the Imám of his garments and carried them away as loot of war. Shimr, who was adamant in his determination to kill all the surviving members of Ḥusayn's family and plunder their possessions, hastened again at the head of a group of soldiers to the tents where the Imám's family were sorely lamenting the grievous loss of their dearest one. But Ibn Sa'd noted this and came up to prevent the massacre of those who survived and were captives in his hands.

The Imám had more than thirty wounds on his body and arms from the swords and spears of his enemies. To leave no trace of the martyrs, the commander ordered his cavalry to trample the corpses with their galloping horses. This done, the heads of the martyrs were raised aloft on long spears. The impoverished members of Ḥusayn's family were roped together and dragged to the bare camels which would carry them to the seat of the governor. Zaynu'l-'Ábidín was put in chains and treated ruthlessly, though he was ill and weak.

So Ibn Sa'd and his victorious army left the plain of Karbilá, which was strewn with the remains of the martyrs, and marched off to Kúfah with immense excitement and joy, anticipating the praise and rewards which the governor had promised.

What agony possessed the hearts of the Imám's family remains forever undescribed. Words and phrases fail any writer who attempts to portray such poignant sorrows in the history of man's atrocities. As the family looked back, they could see the desert strewn with the mutilated bodies of their dear ones; and when they cast their eyes to the road ahead, they beheld nothing but a forest of lances and spears adorned with their heads. Khúlí was the carrier of Ḥusayn's head.[1] The only re-

[1] See *Gleanings from the Writings of Bahá'u'lláh*, section xxxix.

maining son of Ḥusayn was in chains, driven along with the rest of his family to an unknown fate and further humiliations. Their prayer was to gain the approval of their Lord and His acceptance of all they had so generously offered at the altar of faith, devotion and sacrifice.

Before the arrival of the army, Ibn Zíyád had stationed soldiers at various posts on their path to be on guard lest the disastrous condition of the family of the Prophet should drive the masses to revolt. When the inhabitants of Kúfah saw the humiliations heaped upon Ḥusayn's relatives, they wept. Zaynu'l-'Ábidín, seeing their tears, reproached them, saying, "You slaughter the members of our family and now you shed tears!" A woman who was watching from the roof of her house as they passed was so bitterly moved that she brought pieces of cloth and veils to cover the barely-dressed bodies of the sisters and daughters of Ḥusayn.

Zaynab, daughter of 'Alí and sister of Ḥusayn, looked pityingly at the people of Kúfah and addressed them in a tone as vigorous and eloquent as her father's. "O ye inhabitants of Kúfah! O ye people of deceit and dissension! You shed tears, but you do not feel ashamed before the Prophet of God! You raised the worst creature to be your sovereign and slaughtered the best of all men. You brought upon yourselves such disgrace that its effects will remain with you forever. No power can erase the evil consequences of your shameful deeds. Nothing can ever wash from your hands the stains of the sacred blood of the martyrs. The Imám was shield and shelter to all the believers, and the sole interpreter of the revealed words of God. Through him could we find our way to the religion of God."

One of the daughters of Ḥusayn exclaimed, "They took us captive, forced us to ride on bare camels, exposed us to the burning heat of the sun and allowed us no shelter in the desert."

Again Zaynu'l-'Ábidín addressed the watching crowds and, after words of praise and prayer to God, affirmed: ". . . I am the son of the one who exercised patience to the end of his life; to the time when you severed his head from his body. Woe be unto you, O inhabitants of Kúfah! You sent letters of invitation to Ḥusayn. You deceived him and placed him in the hands of his enemies. You helped the oppressors to rule over him. How, then, can you ever face the Apostle of God? What will your answers be when He asks you, 'Why did you kill my people and heap sufferings and tribulation upon the members of my family?'"

That fateful day passed. Then Ibn Zíyád invited

the inhabitants of the town to watch the final scene of this tragedy in which he was the chief actor. Crowds of people assembled in his very large house. It is incredible that some of those who had seats of honour in that court of crimes and cruelty were of the most erudite of the region, venerated and famous for their piety. When all were settled in their places, the governor raised his voice to order that the captives be brought into his presence.

But first, the head of Ḥusayn was carried in and placed at his feet. Unable to control his vindictive satisfaction, the governor began to beat the head with the stick he held in his hand. One of the veteran believers, a companion of the Prophet, was present. When he saw the governor's brutal act he was agitated and overcome by grief, and raised his voice in protest, calling out, "O son of Marjánih! Raise your rod from those lips, for many a time have I seen the Prophet's lips caressing that face with tenderest affection, the while He assured us that Ḥasan and Ḥusayn were His twin trusts to the believers!"

When Zaynab and others of Ḥusayn's family were introduced to the court, not one of them saluted the governor. In anger and contempt, he arrogantly inquired, "Who is that woman?" When told she was Zaynab, the sister of Ḥusayn, he observed, "I praise God that He has disgraced you all and revealed your lies."

Immediately Zaynab answered him in clearest terms. "Praise be to God who honoured us by our relation to the Apostle of God. It is He who cleansed our hearts from the dust of doubts and sin. Know this of a certainty, that the wrong-doers and sinners are placed in disgrace but we are not of them."

"See what God has wrought for your brother and his men," rejoined Ibn Zíyád.

"It was decreed by God that some of the best and dearest ones should give their lives in the path of His religion. Ere long the supreme Judge will call them and you to His presence, and He is indeed the best of all judges," the girl replied.

With mounting rage Ibn Zíyád retorted, "Now that we have killed your brothers, my heart is calm and appeased."

Quietly Zaynab replied, "O son of Marjánih! You uprooted the tree of prophethood and cut off its branches and boughs. We hope that now your heart rests in peace and that your thirst for the blood of our family is quenched."

Ibn Zíyád's glance then fell on Zaynu'l-'Ábidín, and he asked, "Who is he?" The answer came, "'Alí, son of Husayn."

Furiously, Ibn Zíyád exclaimed, "Did not God kill you and your brothers?" And the Imám answered, "The death of each individual is by the decree of God."

In a blaze of wrath the governor ordered that he, too, should be beheaded. Then Zaynab's voice rang through the room: "This is the only male member left to our family. If you desire to kill him, kill all of us together!"

Zaynu'l-'Ábidín looked calmly at Ibn Zíyád. "Do you threaten me with death? Do you not know that martyrdom in the path of God is our prerogative and our greatest aspiration?"

Impatiently, Ibn Zíyád shouted an order to place the members of Ḥusayn's family in the prison adjacent to the mosque. To cause them more suffering, he commanded that the head of Ḥusayn be raised on a spear and carried through the lanes and markets of Kúfah.

After some days, the governor ordered Shimr, accompanied by soldiers and helpers, to conduct the captives to the court of Yazíd in Damascus.

When Yazíd was informed of the approach of the mournful caravan from Mesopotamia he ordered the inhabitants of Damascus to decorate the doors of their homes and shops with all festive ornaments and to prepare themselves to celebrate the victory of his dynasty over Ḥusayn. Crowds gathered outside the gate of the town to watch the arrival of the dejected and afflicted captives, who were preceded by the severed heads of their martyrs. Then came the invalid son of Ḥusayn in chains, followed by all the others, fastened with ropes on the bare-backed camels. As they approached the seat of the tyrant of Syria, the caravan stopped near the great Mosque of Damascus.

Yazíd arranged a very large gathering in his mansion. Seated on his throne and wearing a special crown, he imitated the Persian and Roman Emperors. At his behest the captives were brought into his presence. First came a man who carried the head of Ḥusayn. Reaching the throne of Yazíd, he shouted, "Load my horses with gold and silver. We have killed the noblest son of the most exalted parents."

These complimentary words about the vanquished put Yazíd into a rage; he ordered the immediate death of the offender. In his hoarse, loud voice, he shouted at the culprit, "If you believed they were the noblest, why did you kill them?"

The heads of the martyrs were placed in a row at the feet of Yazíd, with Ḥusayn's in the centre of a glittering tray of gold. The grandson of Abú-Sufyán fixed his gaze upon the heads of Háshim's descendants. Relief and satisfaction were reflected in his face. The long struggle for power was ended, and the Umayyads were safely settled on the throne of their earthly sovereignty.

Then the members of Ḥusayn's family were brought in. As they entered, one of the audience gave vent to his feelings and shouted, "You did well, Yazíd! You exterminated the generation of the Prophet and raised to command the son of an adultress."

Yazíd, intoxicated with his victory over the Háshimites, and remembering the deep-rooted rivalry which the Umayyads had always harboured in their hearts, the jealousy which had always consumed them, could not but express joy at the vengeance his clan had now taken. He wished that his ancestors had lived to behold the avenging sword-strokes on the bodies of the Háshimites, could have viewed with him the members of Ḥusayn's household, now captive in his conquering hands.

Zaynab, watching him, raised her voice fearlessly in exhortation. "Do you realize what you are doing? Though you keep the members of your own family behind curtains and veils, you expose the daughters of the Prophet to public gaze. You carry them from town to town, hold them in bonds and chains, exhibit their sufferings, look at them in anger, feel no shame in killing them, beat the mouth of Ḥusayn with joy . . . Are you followers of the Apostle of God? You rule with the sword of Muḥammad, and are haughty and proud because of this transient sovereignty."

Yazíd turned to Zaynu'l-'Ábidín and said, "Your father challenged my rule."

The Imám replied with quiet force, "Prophethood and kingship are given to our family. Tell me, in whose house were the verses of God revealed? In yours or ours? Did Gabriel descend to your house or to ours? Do the verses commanding respect and reverence for the divine family refer to yours or ours?"

With this, Yazíd attempted to be kind and lenient to the prisoners and sent them into his mansion where all bewailed their condition. He even offered them luxurious hospitality which was not accepted, for scions of the uncompromising Ḥusayn never deigned to curry favour with the despicable tyrant of Syria.

On one occasion, when soldiers began to play their drums and sound their trumpets and bugles, Yazíd said to Zaynu'l-'Ábidín, "This is our regal music". The Imám did not utter a word, but waited until midday when the _adhán_ was sounded.

"This is the song of our family which will endure forever," he told Yazíd.

To win the favour and sympathy of his captives, Yazíd often expressed regret at what had taken place in Mesopotamia, asserting that it had not been by his instruction. He even requested them to adopt Damascus as their abode where all their needs would be met. But Zaynu'l-'Ábidín and his companions asked to return to Medina, the city of the Prophet, by way of Karbilá where they would bury the heads of their dead. As to their needs, they never alluded to any, but asked only that their relics should be returned to them. Those objects of adoration had been entrusted to their grandmother Fáṭimah, the most exalted woman of the Islamic era. Though seemingly small and insignificant, each one of these silent objects conveyed to them assurance of the ultimate victory of the Faith of God, and would impart to the remaining members of the Holy Family the fragrance of love growing in their midst.

They reached the plain of Karbilá on the fortieth day after the martyrdom of Ḥusayn. To their great satisfaction, they found that the devoted members of a tribe called Banú-Asad had courageously gathered the bodies of the martyrs and interred them. Having buried the heads, they offered prayers and resumed their way towards Ḥijáz.

They took the same path as Ḥusayn had followed to Mesopotamia. They paused to watch the rippling Euphrates hasten towards the south, and they remembered those who had thirsted for even one cup of its water. Every pebble of the desert spoke to them of the days just past, and of Ḥusayn, whose brave march across the desert had led him to an apex of glory and spiritual conquest so exalted that none, even of the immortal heroes amongst the Imáms, could ever approach it.

As was said before, to attempt to recount the true story of Ḥusayn resembles the excavating of ancient towns from beneath layers of stone, sand and soil heaped upon them by time and by man. For centuries the pure and stainless life of Ḥusayn has been buried and obliterated under mounatins of false judgement on the part of the enemies of his cause, and by exaggerated accounts from the immature and ignorant among his followers. The little written here falls within the light shed upon Ḥusayn's life by the intense love shown for him by Bahá'u'lláh. This account is short, and very limited in scope, but the hope is that it will frame worthily a picture so exquisite and divine in beauty and grandeur.

Amongst the grandchildren of the Prophet Muhammad, the one who resembled Him most was Imám Husayn. He was of medium height, with an olive complexion. Dignity coupled with charm made him a magnet to whom all were drawn, even unbelievers. The most attractive of all his qualities and heavenly gifts were his bold and resolute eyes and his warm, penetrating and resonant voice which inspired awe and commanded respect. "Hussain, the second son of Ali, had inherited his father's virtues and chivalrous disposition."[1]

Like the Prophet, he loved the poor and destitute. Whatever gifts were brought to him by the believers were distributed among the poor and needy. In fact he was often seen in their humble abodes, sitting with their families in an attitude of natural and sincere love that made every pain-racked soul relieved, happy and proud.

He was the essence of piety. It was his noble and pious life which enhanced his judgement and authority.

Husayn's fame as the most generous man of the Arabian peninsula spread far and wide. If his children were taught verses of the Qur'án, Husayn

[1] Syed Ameer Ali, op. cit., p. 83.

would make a gift of one thousand dínárs to their teacher.

Once a man approached Ḥusayn and requested his financial help. He gave the man enough to sustain himself and his family. He then counselled him with words even more valuable than the coins, asking the man to come to him whenever he stood in further need; and should he choose to approach another, to make sure that his benefactor believed in God, loved his kind, and, above all, was honest and true.

From early childhood Ḥusayn demonstrated such remarkable feats of chivalry, undaunted courage and erudition that people took pleasure in sitting at his feet to learn the heavenly lessons he was endowed to offer. His words were plain and he expressed truth in uncompromising terms. His addresses were concise, cogent and timeless: they stand forever as standards of truth and examples of genuine eloquence.

Many people wrote to Ḥusayn and took pride in receiving his answers to their inquiries. When asked about God, the Imám explained that God could never be comprehended by our senses, nor should He ever be compared with man. God is very near, he explained, but free of attachment. He is remote and aloof, but inseparable from His creation. He is known by His own proofs and identified by His own signs.[1]

He defined the people of the world and their religious beliefs by saying that they are in thraldom to their possessions, riches and luxuries. For many, religion is a word uttered by their tongues; and even when they profess belief, their real interest is to procure and secure a livelihood. When tested, the true believers are very few indeed.

When Abúdhar, one of the early believers in the Prophet Muḥammad and His staunch supporter, was exiled from Medina by order of the third Caliph, 'Uthmán, 'Alí became very sad and, accompanied by Ḥasan and Ḥusayn, went to bid him farewell. 'Alí asked his two sons to say good-bye to their "uncle". Ḥusayn, in that sorrowful moment, said to the exiled believer, "The people withheld their luxuries from you, and you did not sell them your faith. How detached you are from that which was not given you; and how needful they are of what you did not sell them."

When the agent of Mu'áwíyah endeavoured to take the oath of allegiance in favour of Yazíd, he used words as sweet as honey, but, as usual, his words were mixed with the venom of violation of

[1] The Persian mystic poet Rúmí says, "The sun rose. Its rays are its own proofs and its light its own sign."

the covenant of God. Ḥusayn with characteristic audacity and frankness warned the inhabitants of the city of the Prophet against the deeds of those who would lead them away from the true path of God. He declared that they attempted to cover falsehood with the garment of truth. To follow them, one would win this world and all its transient joys, but would surely lose the everlasting life in the Kingdom on high. This is indeed the greatest of all losses that man can sustain.

Ḥusayn made an eternal statement about prayer, the gleaming truth of which will be understood increasingly by mankind as it approaches the age of maturity. He claimed that we should never pray to our Lord and Creator for fear of the tortures of hell, nor because we covet the joys and comforts of paradise. We must worship God, Ḥusayn said, because He is worthy of our praise and adoration.

Some of the believers, more than others, came to realize the magnitude of his rank as the spiritual leader of mankind; they devoted their lives and consecrated their wealth in service to him and sought always to be in his presence. Ibn ʿAbbás was one of the most erudite men of his time, but he used to walk holding the stirrup of Ḥusayn's saddle while the Imám was riding.

Abú-Hurayrah was another of the pious and

learned people of his age. He used to clean the Imám's shoes with his own shirt, saying, "Should the people know what I know of him, they would certainly carry him on their shoulders."

The story of Bilál and his love for Ḥusayn is indeed touching. Bilál was one of the earliest to believe in the Prophet Muḥammad. When the Prophet decided to call the believers to the prescribed prayers, He asked Bilál to go up on the roof and chant the verses of the *adhán*. After the passing of the Apostle of God, he left Ḥijáz for Jerusalem where he made his home. Once Imám Ḥusayn sighed and expressed a wish to hear once more the far-reaching, vibrant and vigorous voice of Bilál. Bilál saw the Prophet of God in his dream summoning him and remonstrating with him as to why he had forsaken His family. On the morrow, Bilál was on his way to Medina. The moment he arrived in the city of his Beloved, he hastened to His resting-place. No sooner had he reached there than he threw himself on that sacred tomb. Overwhelmed with sorrow and drowned in memories of the past, he pressed himself against the grave, crying and shedding bitter tears. When the Imám came to know of his arrival, he immediately went to the holy precincts where he found this faithful friend of his Grandfather. He lifted him up, embraced him with much affection, and surrounded him with compassion and tenderness. He wiped his tears, strengthened and consoled his heart and asked him to go to the mosque and sound the *adhán*. When the believers heard the golden voice of Bilál chanting the first verses of the *adhán* their hearts leaped in their breasts. The middle verses brought them out of their houses; and by the time Bilál had concluded the call to prayer, they were already hastening to the mosque.

In the course of this short account of the Imám's life we have come to know that he never ceased to guide people to the right path of God. Even in that moment when he had fallen from his horse, with his own death fast approaching, when he beheld Shimr and his unruly soldiers about to sack his tents where his family shrank in terror, he called out to them to behave as Arabs, even if not as Muslims.

On this day of his martyrdom, he addressed his friends and foes, urging them to safeguard themselves against the world and its manifold temptations. The world is always encircled by multifarious disasters, he told them. Its bounties vanish soon. Its joys grow dim and clouded. The best of all fortunes in this transient life is to be virtuous, to have the fear of God in one's heart, and to be faith-

ful to God's Messengers, the worthiest and noblest
Beings of the whole creation.

Not only did Ḥusayn, in his lifetime, firmly and
compellingly exhort his friends and followers in
beautiful and eloquent language, but he has remained an ever-glowing, ever-burning beacon of
guidance, a fount of heavenly qualities and spiritual
utterances.

Our account will not be complete without a
tribute to Zaynab, the sister of Ḥusayn. Even now
we can hear the echoes of her lamentations on the
episode of Karbilá ringing throughout the centuries. When the terrible butcheries enacted on
that plain were ended, what emotions must have
surged in the heart of that great and noble lady! In
the hours of loneliness, might she not have whispered to her own soul such words as these: "I
followed my brother and trudged the path of
suffering and sacrifice. He had an inherent gift
which, like a magic spell, commanded respect and
admiration. We followed him and walked in his
shadow and under his shelter. I bore the loss of my
own sons, the loss of my nephews, the loss of my
brother 'Abbás, and the loss of many of the young
believers who, intoxicated by the love of God,

hastened to tear the veils asunder in order to behold the beauty of their Lord and Creator. All these losses could be tolerated, but the loss of Ḥusayn is one which cannot be measured. He was the Imám and we were his followers, enthralled by his love. His grievous loss is a wound so deep that nothing will give us rest or peace.

"I remember the blazing heat of Arabia, the burning thirst of the children, the swift storms which swept sand into our eyes and dust across our parched lips. The winds were sometimes so ravaging that the tents, our flimsy shelters, would be shaken and often nearly swept away. In the stillness of the night, I heard voices of a ferocity no mortal has ever experienced, the howling of rapacious soldiers who could not wait for dawn to break. I saw with my own eyes young enthusiastic youths who offered their souls when embraced and caressed by my beloved brother.

"These giants of spiritual strength were cast down by pygmies moved by lust and greed. How can these weaklings ever fill their places? I was captive in Kúfah and Damascus and saw with my own eyes their tottering earthly rulership. Their triumph came not from a heavenly revelation, nor was it due to any supremacy of courage and devotion. No gentle and continuing effort sustained it;

rather, it was a spiritual disaster that ravaged the whole of the Muslim world.

"Did I endure all these ordeals? Did my eyes behold and my ears hear? How can I live? How am I able to sustain all these tempests of tests and trials? Why am I alive? Why?"

It was decreed by God that Zaynab should live to protect the fourth Imám and thus assure the continuation of the Imamate until the year 260 A.H. She was the one who raised the cry of "Yá Ḥusayn!", and rallied the friends who were faithful, addressing them in a language so eloquent and stormy that it reminded them of Imám ʿAlí. Had it not been for her forbearance in adversity and her incessant efforts to recount the events of those first ten days of Muḥarram, we should not have a full story of the radiant Ḥusayn, the "Prince of Martyrs".

A dramatic and marked contrast exists between the Imám and Yazíd, who left no stone unturned in his efforts to subjugate Ḥusayn. Yazíd was tall, well-built, and had a robust constitution. His hoarse voice when raised in anger created fear in his palace and capital. He was absorbed in luxuries and frivolities and frequently engaged in idle pastimes, displaying a great affection for games and hunting.

In the words of Syed Ameer Ali, "Yazid was both cruel and treacherous; his depraved nature knew no pity or justice. His pleasures were as degrading as his companions were low and vicious. He insulted the ministers of religion by dressing up a monkey as a learned divine and carrying the animal mounted on a beautifully caparisoned Syrian donkey wherever he went. Drunken riotousness prevailed at court, and was naturally imitated in the streets of the capital."[1]

When Ḥusayn rose in defence of the covenant of God and chose the path of sacrifice with longing and enthusiasm, some of the believers, instigated by agents of the Umayyad capital, dared to send him letters of protest, criticizing his action and interrogating him as to why he had become the cause of dispersion by creating innovation in the Faith of God. They even exhorted him to be silent, else he would ignite the fire of mischief.

Ibn Zíyád was, in the beginning, one of the followers of 'Alí; but his appointment by Yazíd as governor of the eastern provinces of the Empire caused him to forget 'Alí and his family and to commit atrocities beyond description.

Ibn Sa'd was the son of an avowed supporter of Islám, the commander who had conquered Persia

[1] op. cit., p. 83.

under the flag of Islám. The promise of the rulership of Ray caused Ibn Sa'd to violate the covenant
of God, and to pride himself on having discharged
the first arrow to strike Ḥusayn.

Those who signed the death-warrant of the
Imám were numbered among the judges, religious
leaders and potentates of the mosques. But as
Gibbon has clearly explained, the temptations were
too great for people to resist; they could not stand
firm and unmoved. Shorayh, the chief judge, was
one who was seated in the government-house of
Kúfah when the heads of the martyrs were brought
into the presence of Ibn Zíyád. With him was the
leader of the congregational prayers, who had won
the admiration of the populace by his reading and
study of the Qur'án, and his prayer vigils at night.
The news of the ignominious death suffered by the
grandson of the Prophet awakened in him no prick
of conscience. As usual, he led the congregation in
prayers and took not the least trouble to ponder
upon what had taken place, nor to understand the
station of the one who had accepted these afflictions
in the path of God.

Shimr, the heartless beast whose mere name
creates waves of horror in the hearts of the faithful,
was one of the religious judges and so apparently
pious that he would pick up thorns from the roads

lest they prick the feet of the pedestrians. Yet it was he who stepped forward in a display of heroism to decapitate the Imám with ten strokes of his heavy sword.

When Ibn 'Uqbah and his Syrian mercenaries reached Medina, the soldiers' greed for the riches of the people, their butcheries, their voluptuousness and unbridled lust proved unlimited. Even the most revered believers, including the veteran companions and helpers of the Prophet, were mercilessly put to death by them. Their horses were tethered and fed in the great Mosque, the ornaments and relics of the shrines were confiscated, and having disastrously ruined the city of the Prophet, they hastened to the Qiblih of Islám in Mecca and caused severe damage to the most holy spot in the Islamic world. These uncontrolled savageries were stopped only by the news of the sudden death of Yazíd. The mercenaries rushed home, but the bitter remembrance of their cruelties remained as a permanent thorn in the hearts of the believers.

This insolent and disrespectful spirit, and this heedlessness towards Islám and its resuscitating powers prevailed throughout the Umayyad dynasty. Exceptions were rare indeed. Al-Walíd II, one of the Umayyad caliphs, was so intoxicated with his worldly power that he tore the Qur'án into pieces, and while singing poems addressed the Book of God in mocking terms: "If God asks you as to who tore His Book, tell Him Walíd".

In the light of these comparisons, let us refer to the statements of 'Abdu'l-Bahá about the destructive influence of the Umayyad caliphs. He gave these explanations at the time of His incarceration in the prison-city of 'Akká (Acre), then governed by rulers many of whom were not less cruel. When asked about the "beast" mentioned in the eleventh chapter of the Revelation of St. John, He replied:

"*The beast that ascendeth out of the bottomless pit shall war against them, and shall overcome them and kill them,*"—this beast means the Baní-Umayyih[1] *who attacked them from the pit of error, and who rose against the religion of Muḥammad and against the reality of 'Alí—in other words, the love of God.*

It is said, "The beast made war against these two witnesses"[2]—*that is to say, a spiritual war; meaning that the beast would act in entire opposition to the teachings, customs, and institutions of these two witnesses, to such an extent that the virtues and perfections which were diffused by the power of those two witnesses among the peoples and tribes would be en-*

[1] Dynasty of the Umayyads.
[2] These two witnesses were the Prophet Muḥammad and Imám 'Alí. (A.-Q.F.)

tirely dispelled, and the animal nature and carnal desires would conquer. Therefore this beast making war against them would gain the victory—meaning that the darkness of error coming from this beast was to have ascendancy over the horizons of the world, and kill those two witnesses:—in other words, that it would destroy the spiritual life which they spread abroad in the midst of the nation, and entirely remove the divine laws and teachings, treading underfoot the Religion of God: nothing would thereafter remain but a lifeless body without spirit.

"And their dead bodies shall lie in the street of the great city...."

... "Their bodies" means the Religion of God, and "the street" means in public view....

... the nations, tribes, and peoples would look at their bodies, that is to say, that they would make a spectacle of the Religion of God: though they would not act in accordance with it, still, they would not suffer their bodies—meaning the Religion of God— to be put in the grave. That is to say, that in appearance they would cling to the Religion of God and not allow it to completely disappear from their midst, nor the body of it to be entirely destroyed and annihilated. Nay, in reality they would leave it, while outwardly preserving its name and remembrance.[1]

[1] 'Abdu'l-Bahá, *Some Answered Questions*, pp. 60–62.

These words epitomized the centuries of the Islamic Era and the disastrous blows the Muslim community suffered throughout its history. Following the sack of Medina, we are told, "Paganism was once more triumphant, and 'its reaction', says a European historian, 'against Islâm was cruel, terrible, and revolting' . . . The colleges, hospitals, and other public edifices built under the Caliphs were closed or demolished, and Arabia relapsed into a wilderness!"[1]

Little did Yazíd know how futile his ephemeral sovereignty would be! Steeped in viciousness, he could not have a clear vision of the future. Gradually the small dim light he had in his heart grew weaker and weaker and was finally extinguished. By his own deeds he rang the death-knell of his own rulership which lasted about four years. Ere the ending of his days and before the lusty songs were terminated, his image was hidden under the pall of death, forever shrouded in shame.

History reversed the tide of events to favour the one who had been so mercilessly wronged. In the course of decades and centuries, Ḥusayn snatched victory from the dreadful jaws of the "beast" which, gradually losing vigour and its hold over the hearts and souls of the people, was left abandoned.

[1] Syed Ameer Ali, op. cit., p. 88.

Great indeed was Ḥusayn's undertaking and hard was the path he had to pursue amidst his ferocious enemies. It was a time of foolish and unfounded beliefs, which proliferated in the favourable climate prepared by the Umayyad dynasty. But to safeguard the faith of his Grandfather, Ḥusayn accepted all atrocities.

As we review the history of those eventful years, we reach a page wherein we behold Ḥusayn's sacrifice emerging to cleave a path through the debris of cruelties and massacre. His figure comes forth from the mist of the past. His story re-echoes in sad and heavenly song. Minstrels wandering from tent to tent and from town to town sing tales of those intrepid souls who severed all their ties with the world, suffered with great tenacity, composure and dignity, and marched on and on, higher and higher, towards an apex which touches the zenith of the heavens of Glory.

POSTSCRIPT

Because of the treacherous acts of those who dared to flout the words of the Prophet Muḥammad, the two centres of Islám—the spiritual and the administrative—were forever separated. While the spiritual centre remained in Ḥijáz where the Qiblih of Islám is fixed, the administrative centre drifted away, shifting from Ḥijáz to Damascus, Mesopotamia, Egypt and, finally, the Ottoman Empire.

This factor, and the attitudes and actions of the caliphs, drained the vitality of the Faith. To retain the caliphate in their own hands, and hereditary in their lineages, they spared no efforts to keep the Muslim world under their sway.

It is not the aim nor is it a part of this essay to analyze the spiritual damage resulting from their deeds, but the writer desires to draw the attention of readers to the fact that such innovations undermined the religion of God and its institutions, thus causing a gradual decline in the morale of its adherents and bringing the institution of the caliphate to its close in the year A.D. 1924, at the hands of that "audacious man", Muṣṭafá Kemál Atatürk.

CPSIA information can be obtained at www.ICGtesting.com
Printed in the USA
245342LV00001B/41/A